How to be

Popular

*Like a Celebrity
And Love it*

☙❧

Building Friendships That Last

How to be

Popular

Like a Celebrity
And Love it

Building Friendships That Last

Joan Wright Lewis

JVP
Published by
Jo-Val Publishing, LLC
Avon, Indiana

www.jovalpub.com

Published by:
JO-VAL PUBLISHING, LLC

Copyright © 2009, by Joan Wright-Lewis
Copyright © 1995, by Joan Wright-Lewis

ISBN: 0-9629832-9-2 (sc)
978-0-9629832-9-0

ISBN: 0-9629832-0-9 (hc)
978-0-9629832-0-7

This book is printed on acid free paper
Printed and bound in the United States of America

Cover Design: Jo-Val Publishing
Interior Design: Joan Wright Lewis
Illustrations: Joan Wright Lewis

Dedicated to Alexia, and Nastassja my beautiful daughters, my lovely niece Ashley Wright; and to Wycham Lewis, my handsome husband, whose encouragement, support, love and wisdom guided me through.

Smile you are gifted and smart

True love can be found only in <u>Jesus</u>.

𝒴ou are Irreplaceable

CONTENTS

Contents

Contents

Our childhood experiences have produced who we are today.

ACKNOWLEDGEMENTS

Special thanks go to the following:

My mother, Etta Wright, for all the good things she taught me.
My husband, Wycham Lewis, for his love and care.

Editors:

Winsome Lewis
Ann Marie Simmond

Patrick M. Roe

All my friends who prayed for this production

Everyone who submitted their beautiful photos.

Alan Heuss
Alexia Lewis
Alice Kobba
Angelee Crawford
Ann-Marie Dawes
Ashley Steffen
Ashley Wright
Charles Wright
Larry Nicholas

Nastassja Lewis
Natasha Alyce Taylor
Phillip R. Mann
Rachel Phillips
Robin Heuss
Savannah White
William Smith
Wycham Lewis

ഇ)രു

ഇ)രു

Everyone is born
with one or more
talents. That
includes you.

A NOTE FROM THE AUTHOR

Y ou are unique, special, and wonderfully made. Never think that any one is better than you. We all have talents, and some people are more talented than others. However, each person utilizes his or her talent in an exceptional way. Everyone is born with one or more talents. That includes you. If you are quiet and reserved and you want to be popular, study the popular people. Be yourself, but realize that there are certain principles that govern such popularity. Never sell yourself short to please anyone. Be honest and forgiving. The things you do in life have a way of coming back to you, so be good to others.

You are Unique

INTRODUCTION

ave you ever noticed that people who are popular and likeable have a certain charisma that draws people to them? Perhaps they know a lot of people or perhaps they are very friendly. However, they all have one thing in common – they are well known by the majority.

Some people are popular because they are in the limelight. Perhaps they are celebrities, politicians or leaders. However, there are others that are not in the main stream who are also popular. These individuals are caring, helpful, friendly, have a great sense of humor, and always do the right thing for others.

*Y*ou are Unique, and wonderfully made.
You are beautiful.

God will see us through

God, You see us through everything we do.

You see us through bad situations too.

You see us through when we are down.

Because You love us, You pick us up and put our feet on higher ground.

You see us through things we do not deserve.

Because You love us, and see us through, we will always love you.

By Nastassja Lewis

$\mathcal{I}$f you tend to have a happy disposition or you are optimistic about life, you most likely had a happy, satisfied childhood.

Part I

When you are popular, you are widely liked and favorable.

There are two kinds of popularity:
1. Negative popularity. (being unpopular)
2. Positive popularity.

First, we will look at negative popularity. By eliminating all negatives first, we can focus on the positives.

$\mathcal{P}$eople who are popular and likeable have a certain charisma that draws people to them

22

We are creatures of adaptation. We are constantly going through periods of adjustment and changes in order to grow. Some of our traits that are formed may be disliked by others and us. However, we have the ability to make changes in our lives.

Our childhood experiences have produced who we are today. They have molded our thoughts, words and actions. If you are unpopular, you owe it to yourself to look very deeply into your childhood experiences. If you tend to have a positive disposition and are optimistic about life, you most likely had a happy, satisfied childhood. If you are negative, resentful, or gloomy, you may have experienced unhappiness throughout your childhood more often than enjoyable times. Try to find your way back and sort out the reasons for your unpleasant thoughts. Forgive any wrongs done to you. Forgiveness does not set the person free from the wrongs they did to you. It sets you free to

be happy and to live your life abundantly. You are worth it.

Think about this story of a young man named Dave. Dave was unhappy most of the time as a child. Along with being unhappy, someone hurt and embarrassed him enormously when he was young. As a young adult, he was angry. If anyone crossed his path and showed any signs or actions of those who hurt him when he was a child, he lashed out at them in rage. One day, Dave met a good friend. She talked to him and advised him to forgive what had happened. It took him a long time to do this. One day, he finally forgave the person who wronged him, plus the other people that made him unhappy when he was a child. Dave felt free deep down inside. He was filled with emotions, and his life changed that day. Dave thanked God for giving him the power to forgive. He was also grateful for his girlfriend's prayers and advice.

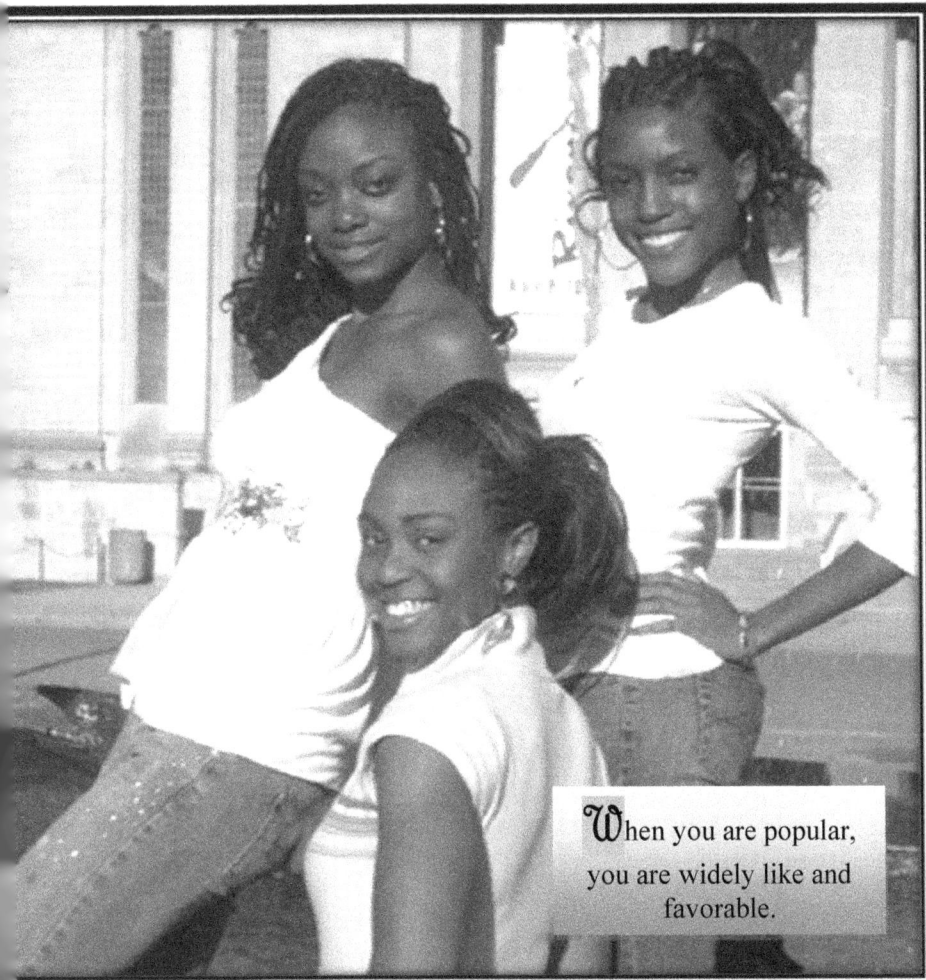

When you are popular,
you are widely like and
favorable.

25

NEGATIVE
POPULARITY/UNPOPULAR

npopular people are often disliked and/or feared. People prefer to be around people that are nice, honest, friendly, funny, and interesting. Below are some traits that are noticeable among those who are unpopular. If some of these traits are part of your personality, it is best to discontinue them.

Rudeness/Offensiveness

Rude and offensive people are shunned. No one wants to be around a rude individual. You may be considered rude for any or all of the following reasons. You:

- always have something sarcastic to say
- talk loudly above everyone
- laugh at people because they are different or do things differently
- slam the door behind you in someone's face
- pick your teeth at the table or make loud noises with your mouth while eating.
- do not return a smile for no apparent reason
- push others out of the way in order to pass
- cut in front of someone who was waiting to go ahead (in a parking space, line, etc.)
- do not respond when asked a question for no perceptible reason

- use curse words around others

- frequently show up late without explanation

- roll your eyes at someone for no noticeable reason, except that you are jealous

- always disrupt a conversation to get your point across

- play loud music that disturbs the quietness, especially at night, with no consideration for others

- yell at others

- always say "shut up" instead of nicely saying "be quiet, please"

- do not know how to say "please" and "thank you"

- say the worst things you can think of to hurt someone's feelings

- force someone to do something they do not want to do

- put others down to make yourself feel good or to prove a point

- pick fights to let yourself look good

- continuously stare at someone

- are frequently concerned with someone else's business

- are a liar

- are a thief

- complain all the time

- are overly argumentive

- have a foul body odor and/ or bad breath due to poor hygiene habits

𝒫eople prefer to be around those who are interesting.

➢ overlook people because they are of a different race, and/or do not look the same as you, etc.

➢ are very sensitive in that you always want to fight someone to get things settled, instead of discussing it

➢ never stop to listen. You always want to state your point, even when you are wrong.

These are only a few of the commonly manifested forms of rudeness and offensive behavior. There are many others. Perhaps you can think of a few to add to this list. If you are rude, you will be well known by this type of behavior, and this could make you unpopular. Good, intelligent people do not want offensive folks around. People who meet any of the points on this list should think about readjusting their personality.

Meddlesome

Are you always meddling in the affairs of others? This is very irritating. Most people, including you, desire some form of privacy. Make yourself busy by reading a good book or volunteer your services by helping others in the church, school or community. Mind your own business. A prying attitude may cause unpopularity.

Cursing

Not everyone uses curse words. In fact, it is very offensive to non-users. Sometimes men curse but do not curse around women. It is not uncommon to see men cursing amongst themselves, only to apologize or modify their speech when a woman passes by. However, men sometimes do not apologize unless a woman looks at them disapprovingly and excuses herself, or explains to them that she does not appreciate those words spoken in her presence.

Lately, it seems that people are saying obscene words around anyone, even in the workplace. This could be due to people lowering their standards by cursing freely. It is distasteful to hear men or women cursing. People tend to look down on those who consistently use offensive language. Women or girls do not realize how offensive it is to use cursewords, and the pedestal that they were placed on is swept from underneath their feet.

Obscene words repeated often over the years could corrupt the mind and conceal the good qualities that you have. It may attract the wrong company and push those away from you who would respect and care for you. Your mouth, lips, and tongue were created in an awesome fashion for expressions of wisdom and beauty. So, choose your words carefully and think before you speak. You are more precious than you could ever imagine.

Your mouth, lips and tongue were created in an awesome fashion for expressions of wisdom and beauty.

Mean Expression

A mean expression is often associated with a bad mood or insecurities. Others may think that you are depressed or angry. When you are around people or approach them, they may look the other way or even fear talking to you.

Has anyone ever said to you, after he or she became acquainted with you, "I thought you were stuck on yourself," or, "At first I thought you didn't like me," or even, "It took me a while to realize you were nice." Practice wearing a pleasant facial expression; it will work wonders! Often, because of stress, resentment or fear, we are completely ignorant of the negative messages we are transmitting with our faces.

A mean expression is often associated with a
bad mood or insecurities.

Aggression

Portraying an aggressive personality may drive people from you. No one likes to be stomped on or shouted at. Why would anyone like to be around someone who is always intimidating and hostile? It would be miserable. People avoid aggressive personalities like the plague.

Bossy

Do you know anyone who likes to order people around, telling them what to do, how to do, and where to go, especially in a pushy manner? This creates resentment and can make the person guilty of this type of behavior unpopular. This is especially true if this bossy person is a woman.

In general, people usually know what to do and can get by on their own. Most of the time a person will ask for specifics if the need arises. When a person needs instruction, it is best to present it in a pleasant and helpful manner.

Very Talkative

A talkative person who never gives others a chance to speak is very annoying. People will try to avoid this individual so they do not have to listen to him or her. It is rude to dominate the entire conversation as if you are a minister on a pulpit. Slow down and actually listen to what others have to say. You may learn something wise!

Gossip

Do not say bad things about others. It most definitely will get back to them and cast you in a negative light. You could lose a friend or an acquaintance. Even if word does not get back to her, you should put yourself in the other person's place. How would you like someone to say bad things about you and tarnish your reputation? Whatever jealousies or insecurities you have, try working on loving who you are. No one is better than you are. Stop putting others down or talking about them!

Servitude

When you do everything people ask you to do, you will be taken advantage of. Your efforts will not be appreciated and you may be disrespected. Of course, everyone will want to be your friend so they can use you as a footstool. However, this kind of popularity is not desirable. You can lose your-self-worth. Remember, you are precious.

Mean Attitude

A mean attitude may bring you popularity, but not the kind you desire. Everyone detests meanness, and no one enjoys the company of an unpleasant person. This attitude robs you of the marvelous opportunities that abound for upholding fine, lasting friendships.

A smile with a pleasant expression works wonders

Do not be the victim of a nasty attitude. Develop a sweet disposition. Spread sunshine. You will feel better inside, the rewards will be numerous, and you will gain many friends.

Smoking/Alcohol

Smoking is a big turn off. It leaves your hair, clothes, and breath with an offensive odor. It spoils a pleasant atmosphere. When that odor is mixed with alcohol, the effect is even more repulsive. It is not pleasant to be around someone who smells nauseating. There are many people, who do not smoke, and hate to be around it. Smoking can cause lung cancer, asthma, shortness of breath, and other very serious health problems. It may even take your life.

Alcohol can destroy your life and your family. Drunk drivers have caused many deaths through careless impaired driving. It has caused terrible grief to innocent families. These drunk drivers are the very same teens, young adults, and grownups who said they would never do anything like that. Now they are serving long sentences in jail and may never recover from the guilt that they feel. Yet, they misjudged themselves while hanging out with friends or having fun at a party, dinner, or nightclub. Do not let it happen to you. Stay away from alcohol. **If you drink, stop.** Get help. Ask God to deliver you from this evil. If you do not drink or smoke, **do not** start; you may regret it in the end.

Know it all

A *know-it-all* attitude is always unwelcome. No one knows everything. If you think you do, you are in a dream world. You are only human. Only God knows everything and is always right. Be open and receptive to new ideas and knowledge. You may not believe or agree with the other person, but sometimes it is always good to listen. You may learn new

You are
more precious
than you
could ever
imagine.

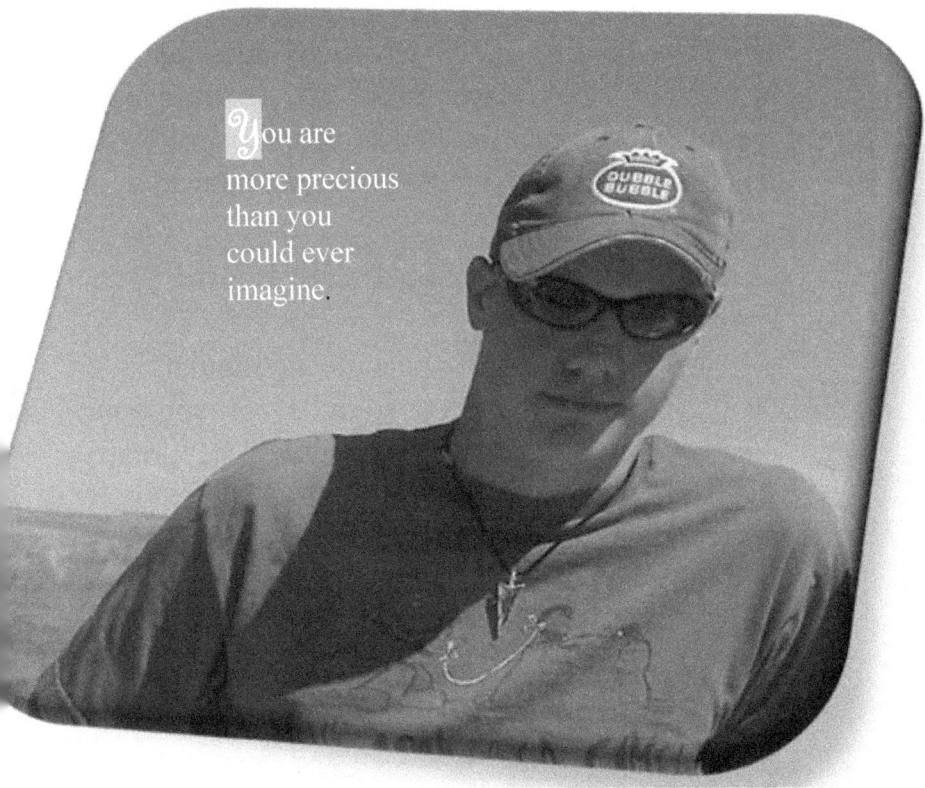

things that you never knew before. At times, you may be absolutely, positively sure that you are right, but you may be unknowingly mistaken. Being Mr. or Ms. *Know-it-all* could cost you precious friends and acquaintances.

Stealing a Boyfriend/ Girlfriend

A quick way to become unpopular is to steal or flirt with your friend's, or someone else's, significant other. You will be greatly disliked, lose good friends, and are likely to regret such actions later. Remember, "What goes around comes around."

Loud mouth/bad jokes

Loud, boisterous people are never generally welcomed in a civilized society. If you talk very loudly, tell off-color jokes, and are always a tattletale, you will be shunned. No one likes to be embarrassed. You may think you look good, but normally people will not tell you how uncultured or stupid you appear.

You must treat yourself with love and
respect, because you are worth it.

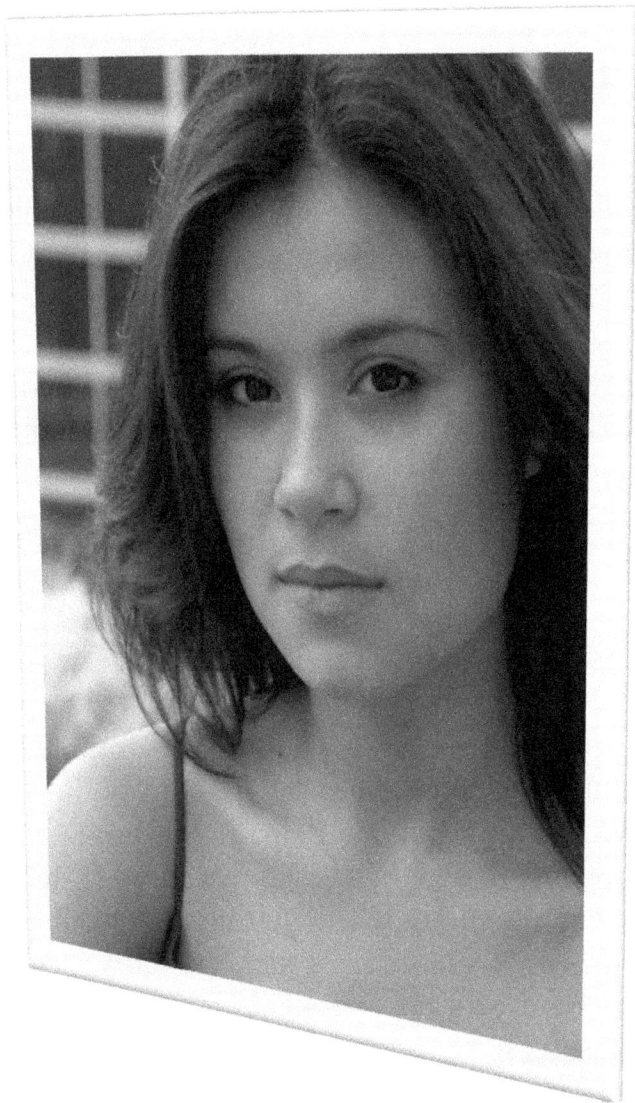

Flattery

Insincere compliments will **not** make you popular. Saying things to a person about himself, that are not completely true, in order to be liked or noticed is flattery. If you like to flatter, eventually your insincerity will be detected and you will not be trusted or liked. In fact, it will become annoying. This practice is sometimes referred to as "kissing up" to someone.

Getting into Trouble

If you are always getting into trouble, you should seek counseling, ask for help, and pray to God, asking Him for help in overcoming this problem. Not everyone knows how to handle someone who is always getting into trouble, so they will avoid him or her, partially because they are afraid of getting into trouble themselves.

Simply take notice, not everyone is getting into trouble. You are probably doing something that is getting you into trouble. Slow down and think positive.

Stop hanging out with troublemakers. This is very important. They are not your friends. They are selfish and pretend to care about you to get what they want accomplished. Take time out for you. Treat yourself with love and respect, (value) because you are worth it. Love yourself. You must think about this. Love you! The powerful God up above said to "Love your neighbor (others) as yourself." Therefore, you cannot love others if you do not love yourself. When you love others, you want the best for them. When you love yourself, you want the best for you in an unselfish way.

Take time out, relax, and think about what you want to become. The world is waiting for you to choose your career so that you can prove yourself to those who said you could not do it. So, what do you want to become; is it an attorney, a politician, an actor, a model, a writer, a plumber, a good parent, a psychologist, a news anchor, a nurse, a photographer, an artist, a consultant, a scientist, neurosurgeon, an archeologist, a publisher, a minister, a teacher, an electrician, a secretary, a professor, or a computer technician. These are just examples of the many choices that are available. Do not be afraid to explore all of your options. Do you want to own your own business? What are you waiting for? Thousands of teens, young adults, and individuals own their own businesses. Therefore, you have the ability to do the same. *Get to stepping!* Stop holding back and move forward with the help and direction of God. Just know, it may not be easy. However, you have the God- given ability to do it. Use your talents, knowledge, education, and skills and go for it. Persevere, persist, and stick with it!

By treating yourself with love and respect, you will learn to treat others with care and kindness. If people do not treat you with love and respect, remember, they are unhappy with who they are. Look for family and friends who are moving upward and who care about

$\mathcal{L}$ook for friends and family who are moving upward and who care about you.

you. Drop friends who are pulling you down, even if it is family.

Picking on People

Avoid "picking" on people; they will dislike you and find you annoying. Remember, "Do unto others as you would have them do to you." Life has a way of repeating itself. If you bully or mistreat others, you may be the one who will be mistreated by someone else in the future. The very person you mistreated or picked on may save your life one day, or may be the one coming your way with a gun for revenge. This world is insane at times, so be good to others. If you feel you have a problem, talk to someone, especially to God. He loves you.

𝒲hatever jealousies or insecurities you have, please work on loving who you are. No one is better than you. You are precious.

Sex

Never use sex to gain popularity. This could upset your life. This is true for males as well as females. You could develop habits that you wish you never had. These tendencies could destroy a good relationship with the opposite sex and cause you pain and anguish. Many risks come with premarital sex. Some includes sexual transmitted diseases and unwanted pregnancy.

Stay away from pornography, especially if you are prone to sexual behaviors that will hurt you and others. Here is a true saying I heard from childhood, "By beholding we become changed." Please be careful what you put into your precious mind.

Learn to abstain from sex if you are not married, and if you are married remain true to your spouse (Exodus 20:14). Sex is a beautiful gift given to us from God for marriage. Put your energy into other worthwhile activities. If you are having trouble with sex, ask God to deliver you. He created sex. He understands human weaknesses. He is willing and waiting to do the best for you. Trust Him; He will work things out for you. If it seems like it is taking a long time, continue believing. Every time temptation arises, tell God you are giving it to Him. Even though you may want to do it badly, give it to God. He said He will never fail you. You may save yourself from a world of trouble, unhappiness, and embarrassment.

If you are being sexually molested or raped, you must seek help. Even, if this happened a long time ago. Talk to a counselor in school, a police officer, the principal, a teacher, a trusted friend, a parent, a minister. Ask God to lead you to the right person that could help you. If the first person did not help, then go to another person until you get the help. Pray to God for help and deliverance. You are precious and no one should be hurting you. This is not normal. Ask God to give you freedom from the person or persons responsible for this crime against you.

If you are the person responsible for this evil crime against someone, you must stop and get help. You are hurting and destroying an innocent person. Turn your life over to God and ask Him to deliver you from these evil thoughts and actions. You will have to give an account to God for your actions. You will face God in the end.

Fault Finding

Are you always finding fault with others? Do you have the tendency to put others down or get angry with them because they do not live up to your expectations? Well, you have a habit that destroys or hurts people's lives and their happiness.

Before you decide to judge someone or find fault with insignificant matters, check yourself first. Your findings may surprise you. You may find that your faults are much more than you think. Do not put others down to make yourself feel good. People who do this usually have an underlying problem (Read Matthew 7:1-5). If you feel you do not have a problem, then realize that when you hurt an individual you drive them from you. This may destroy that person's life, especially if he/she is a child. This can make you very unpopular, and this habit can punch holes in a very good relationship.

54

You need to lighten up and realize that all of us are in this sinful world together and that no one is perfect. In the same way, you want others to treat you with patience, love, and understanding, you should treat others likewise.

If you know someone who is always finding fault, pray for that individual and ask God to change their life. Do not forget to pray for yourself, just in case you are a fault-finder too.

$\mathcal{A}$ blank uninteresting expression may turn people off.

Part II

Minor Negative Personality Traits

𝓘f you are unknown or not popular, do not be alarmed. This may be your choice. You may prefer a quiet, peaceful existence. If you want to be popular or recognized, and you remain invisible, you may have one or more of the following traits:

Too Quiet

Quiet, timid people who have nothing to say are often overlooked or forgotten. People do not usually remember quiet people. They <u>seem</u> uninteresting and boring and people tend to go for the more interesting type. Notice the emphasis on the word "seem." This does not mean that if you are quiet that you are boring and uninteresting. A quiet person *may appear* that way. If you are shy and quiet, do not be afraid to raise your head. Look up instead of looking down at the ground. Smile, you are smart, special, and unique.

Loner/wallflower

If you stand off in a corner alone or hang out alone you are easily forgotten. Staying home all the time will make you unknown.

A smile enhances the looks and adds years to your life.

Get out and go places where you can meet people and make friends. Go to the library, church, school cafeteria, or bookstore. Become more knowledgeable about current events. Read newspapers, magazines, books, and the internet. Watch the news. You could use the information to start conversations with people.

Not smile

☹

A person that never smiles is usually ignored by others. People generally do not take the chance to smile with that person, for fear they might be embarrassed. A smile enhances the looks and adds years to your life. Look in the mirror and practice your smiles.

Always Suspicious

Are you always suspicious of people? Not everyone is out to get you. If you feel this way, you need to talk to a counselor and to God. Suspicious people tend to stay away from

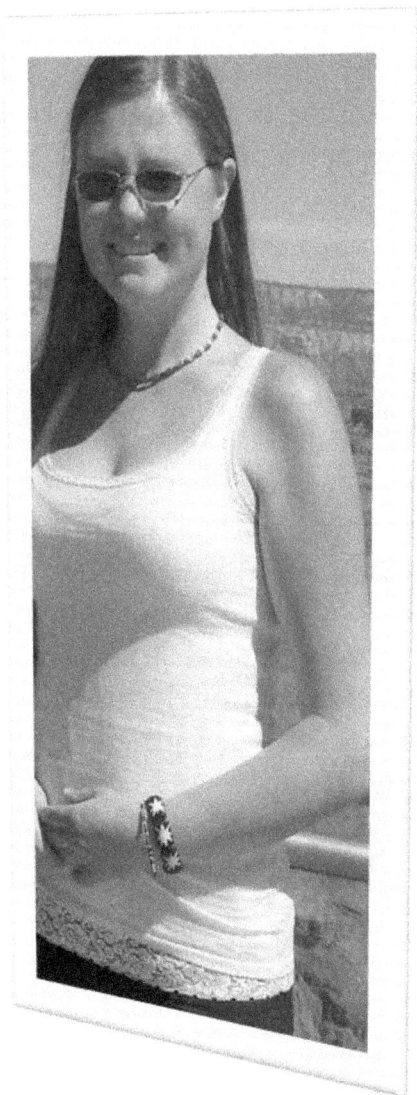

Smile; there is nothing in this world that you cannot overcome through God.

others. If you are inclined to always feel suspicious or are prone to anxiety, remember: things work out for the best, and there is nothing in this world that you cannot overcome through God.

Reaction

Suppose you are telling a joke or you get excited about something, and the person you are talking to shows a blank, uninterested expression. How do you feel? When a person is saying something that is interesting, funny or exciting, it is a good idea to react so they know you care or understand and that you are at least listening. Respond accordingly to the person's emotions. You can drive that person away by being cold. What they see is a boring, uninteresting and unfeeling person. Reactions are important in learning to be popular.

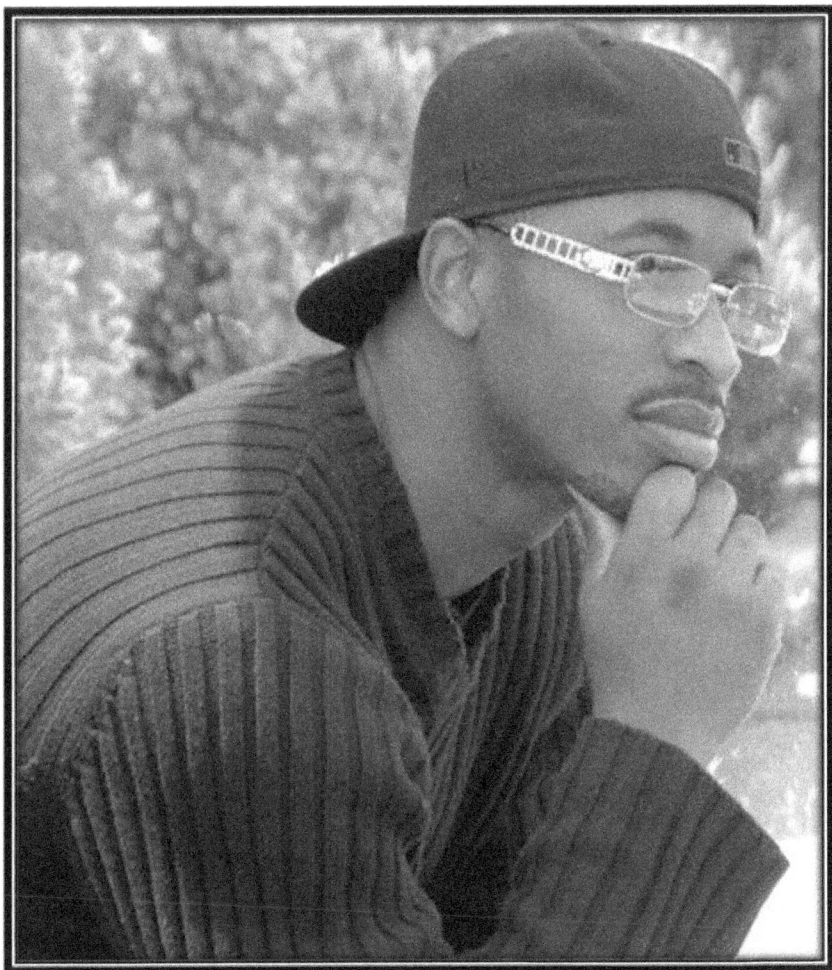

You are handsome, intelligent, sharp and not a follower

63

Clothes & Neatness

When appearing in public try to dress neat and clean. Also, dress modern and for the occasion. You will feel better about yourself and will not be embarrassed around others.

Ladies, it is always a good idea to have a black dress, a red dress, white blouse, two pairs of jeans, black slacks, a black or blue skirt, a black, brown, or blue suit jacket, white T-shirts, sneakers, black shoes, a pair of black boots and matching accessories.

Gentlemen, it is also a good idea to have two white shirts, two pairs of jeans, a pair of dress pants, a dark blue and black suit, white T-shirts, sneakers, black shoes and a black or brown belt. These are the basics and will start you out for any occasion.

64

Pull Up Your Pants, Stay in School

Attention young men: pull up your pants! It looks unbecoming, indecent, and uneducated. You are not only disrespecting yourself, but everyone around you because your appearance is showing that it is okay for everyone to walk around in his or her underwear. Showing your underwear makes a person look as if they have no class. It is not sexy, and looks nasty. You have become a copycat and a spectacle. You do not have a mind of your own. No one wants to see your underwear.

Real men dress like men. This shows that they are sophisticated and have good taste. Appearing and acting as a gentleman opens the door for high-paying jobs, a nice girlfriend, and good friends. When you persistently try to *destroy* your manhood, by wearing your pants below your butt and show your undergarments, like a toddler, society will try to forget you. In addition, there are others in our society who want you to continue wearing your pants down. They look down on you and hope you do not change. They hope you continue dressing indecent, drop out of school, stay in that state of mind for the rest of your life and set the same example for your sons to follow. Somehow, it seems like their wish is being honored.

Girls and women do not want to see their men dressing weak. Just think how distasteful it is to them to see you with your large pants hanging off your behind. To make matters worse, the manly, sexy stride you used to have is ruined. You have to walk a certain way in order to keep your pants up. How would you like to see your mother, your sisters, your girlfriends, your daughters or wives walking down the street with their jeans or skirts hanging off their behind and showing their underwear? Then, in order to keep their jeans or skirts from falling they started to walk weird. Now, imagine how distasteful you look to others. Hello!

You are an awesome human being, made in the image of the Almighty King of the Universe. Wearing your clothes a certain way, makes a difference how you feel about

You are an awesome human being, made in the image of the Almighty King of the Universe.

yourselves. Begin to think of yourself as better than you normally do. You are handsome, intelligent, smart, and you are not a follower. You have what it takes to become the best of what, and who you are. You were built to soar like an eagle; not to peck around like a little chicken! Consider the eagle as he soars through the sky. He moves with confidence and beauty. A chicken can never match up to an eagle.

Wear clothes to accentuate you and your body type. If you wish to wear roomy clothing, then buy African clothes. The styles are comfortable and roomy, yet attractive and decent.

Please, wake up and follow your dreams. It will not be easy. Nothing grand or good comes easy. But, you must keep at it, and never give up. It will happen. As President Barack Obama said in his first address to Congress, *"dropping out of high school is no longer an option. It's not just quitting on yourself, it's quitting on your country - and this country needs and values the talents of every American."* This includes you. We all need your talents. If you dropped out of school, find your way back to school or get your GED.

Do not listen to those who do not want you to move forward in life. They do not like you. They may say they do or pretend to like you, but they are all for themselves.

If you are in school, finish and graduate. **If you are in school, finish and graduate.** If you are in school, finish and graduate. No, this was not a misprint or typo! STAY IN SCHOOL AND GET YOUR DIPLOMA! **IT WILL BE VERY HARD TO GET A DECENT JOB WITHOUT YOUR DIPLOMA.** You also need a diploma to get into college. Please do not say you are not going to college. I told you not to say, "I'm not going to college." You **MUST** go to college. You **must** do your best to go to a junior college or a community college or university. Find and talk to someone who did not graduate from high school or did not go to college. Then talk to someone who did graduate from college or a university. Ask them questions. I promise there will be a vast difference in lifestyle and income. Of course, not all circumstances are the same. However, you will be very happy you did <u>not</u> give up, and you stuck with it and graduated.

You are more precious than gold, diamonds or money. You can never, never be replaced. You have a talent. It is a gift from God to you. Maybe you have more than one talent. God gave it to you so you could use it to make a living, be successful, and bless someone's life. Remember, you are on God's mind. He loves you tremendously and wants the best for you.

Eye to Eye Contact

Do not be afraid to make eye contact with people when they are talking to you. Try your best to look interested. You will allow the person to feel more confident and gain more interest in you. Look them straight in the eyes even if they are boring, but do not stare. Blink, look away and look at them again. You will keep their attention and they will like to be around you. However, if they are boring do not be afraid to excuse yourself kindly and suggest this book to them (in a nice way of course!).

70

Chuck dances on skates. He has auditioned, and has been selected for music videos, movies and other public assignments. He has been seen nationwide and worldwide in music videos. He was featured in the Disney Movie "Enchanted," as one of the dancers on skates. See him on: www.usafree.ws/play

A pleasant expression not only makes you feel good inside, but it makes you better looking.

Part III

POSITIVE POPULARITY

Always smile. ☺ People will remember you for smiling. It brightens your face and breaks down the wall of fear, separation, unkindness or even jealousy. A smile goes a long way. It can brighten someone's day. It can even start a conversation. You could get a date. So smile.

A pleasant expression will draw people to you. It will remove fear from the person looking at you. You will also be better looking.

The fact that a woman looks beautiful does not make her any different from a *plain-* looking woman. So go ahead and talk to her.

Proper Greeting

It is good to greet people. It does not matter where you are – at work, at school, or at play. While passing others, you should say "Hi," or "Hi, how are you?" etc. When you make the acquaintance with others continuously, they will remember you. Even those who do not respond to your greeting will remember you. People will remember you when you recognize them. This is very important.

If people do not respond to your greeting, do not take it personally. Usually people will respond if you keep trying. There might be a number of reasons underlying non-verbal response. Their thoughts may be far away, even though they are looking directly at you. They may also be fearful or may not understand why you are greeting them. Just continue on your way joyfully in your heart and realize that you are of great value. However, be careful of strangers you greet and hold conversation with. Use your discretion. If you feel uneasy about the person, excuse yourself and leave immediately. It does not matter how good looking and trusting he/she may <u>seem</u>. If you feel something is not right, obey your feelings. It is better to be safe than sorry.

Greeting or talking to many people in a good pleasant manner will get you on the road to being popular and respected. Also, remember not to discriminate or be afraid because of nationality, race, sex orientation, religion, or gender. Try going out of your way to talk or be nice to someone you would not normally converse with.

If you are a single man interested in a beautiful female but are fearful or embarrassed to meet her, ask a friend to introduce you. However, you can be brave and introduce yourself. If you do not try, you may miss what might have been a good friendship.

Lance saw a gorgeous young woman at his church one afternoon. He was dying to meet her. She had the most beautiful brown eyes, full soft lips and smooth brown skin. He asked his friends if they knew her. Three of his friends knew her. He asked them to introduce him to her. They agreed. He was introduced to her that evening. He was embarrassed to ask her for her phone number. He asked one of his friends to ask her if it was okay to get her number. She agreed that he could get her number and call her. His friend gave him the number and he called her. To make a long story short, they are now happily married.

The fact that a woman looks beautiful does not make her any different from a *plain*-looking woman. So go ahead and talk to her. If she ignores you, consider it <u>her</u> loss. Perhaps she is not worth your time. There are other women around.

$\mathcal{I}$f you are a single man, interested in a beautiful female and are fearful or embarrassed to meet her, ask a friend to introduce you. She may be your future wife.

To Men: Once you meet a woman, it is absolutely best that you do not say anything foolish to try to impress her. Be yourself and give honest compliments. Do not pry into her personal life. Tell her a little about you. You may ask her if she has a hobby, or what she likes to do. If current events are a good topic, maybe you can talk about it if she does not mind.

Women love to be complimented on their looks, talents, and their hair. Be in awe of her without overdoing it. When she compliments you, let her know you accept and appreciate it. Please do not mention certain body parts; it can be a turn off. If you are interested in her, look into her eyes instead of watching other women passing by. Do not stare at her.

A woman likes a man who is strong (shows strength) and protective; however, please be kind and gentle. Sweet and gentle words works wonders. You may win her heart.

Even though you may be nervous, be sure of yourself, because you are exceptional and amazing. Be in command of who you are. You are a man and wonderfully made by the great Creator. Remember, a woman is all dressed up to feel good about herself, and to get your attention.

Once you have become friends, do not forget, birthdays, Valentines, Christmas, flowers, sweet gentle words and firm, yet gentle touches (very important).

To Women: If a man is brave enough to approach you and you are not interested for one reason or another, be honest and kind. Let him know it was nice of him to stop by, but you are not interested. If he insists or he continues to stay, let him know you are serious and that it has nothing to do with him personally but you are not interested. If he persists, you have the right not to talk to him or to move to another safe area.

Do not feel obligated to speak to someone just because he approached you. If your heart and mind say no, it is probably best to obey, even if he is nice looking. A well-dressed man

$\mathcal{M}$en love when a woman is feminine. It is the opposite of them. They may not say it but they are watching and it makes them feel physically powerful, and manlier.

with a nice looking face and body has nothing to do with the way a man treats a woman.

If you feel good about him and are attracted to him, compliment and admire his masculinity. He will appreciate it. Since you know nothing about him, you may compliment his physical being such as his toned muscles, facial hair, and his clothes. Compliment his masculine manner, such as his walk, the way he looks at you, the way he moves his head, or his smile. Once he begins to speak about himself, listen intently and admire what he is saying and the way he is involved in what he is saying. Do not dominate the conversation. If you met him before or you know him, you have more to marvel at. Admire his manly traits. Be in awe of him without overdoing it.

Now, do not forget to be feminine (girl-like). Men love when a woman is feminine. It is the opposite of them. They may not say it, but they are watching and it makes them feel physically powerful, and manlier. If you act as tough as he does, or compete with him, he will treat you like one of the guys, and more than

likely may not see you as a love interest.
However, he may use you only for a sex partner.
If you are a martial arts expert or a sportive
woman, you can still be feminine and
enchanting.

Do not put him down or call him names
such as stupid, idiot, dummy, dog, not smart,
shorty, big head, or pin head. Hello: this will
eventually turn him off! Say or learn masculine
words such as big guy, tall, handsome, big bear,
you're the man, tough guy, man instead of boy,
smart, intelligent, etc.

Before you go on any date, it is always a
good idea to ask God for His protection. If you
feel uneasy about your date, you are probably
right. God gave us gut feelings of uneasiness
for our protection. Many times, it is best to
listen to them, even if he sweet-talks you. Also,
this is VERY IMPORTANT; watch your juice,
drink, or soda. Do not accept a drink from
strangers. If someone you know out of nowhere
gives you a drink in kindness, do not drink it.

$\mathcal{D}$o not be afraid to talk to a beautiful woman

As was mentioned in part one, do not use sex to be popular. Never jump into bed with a guy if you just met him. Sex should be reserved for marriage. Many women believe that in order to keep a man, they have to give into sex. That is far from the truth. If he cares about you, he will wait.

Men react to and are attracted by sight. When humans (male or female) see pretty things it makes them feel good inside and no one likes to feel bad. Men like to see you dress nice, so do not be afraid to dress pretty. Looking attractive does not mean to dress skimpy and show your breasts popping out and butt cheeks beaming in the light. Please dress decent so you will not look like an easy prey.

Men love when a woman acts sweet and adorable instead of tough and mannish. He also loves when you let him feel like a man. (If you want more information about this subject, go to www.jovalpub.com and sign up for the "Secrets to a Romantic Relationship" Tele-seminar.

Schools and libraries abound with excellent materials. When you possess a wealth of knowledge you will be a more interesting person.

Name

Always try to remember someone's name. It makes them feel special. You can remember their name by repeating it after you hear it. Additionally, you could associate the name with someone or something. If you like the name, you should also compliment the person about it.

A good honest compliment assures you the luxury of popularity, but do not overdo it: the recipient can be embarrassed. Incidentally, a person's name is his/her identity, and they do not mind hearing their name. You must try your best to pronounce it correctly.

Office

You could run for public office. Even if you do not win, you will be well known and familiar with people. If you are part of an organization or school, there are usually offices opening yearly. Some of the offices available are president, vice president, treasurer, secretaries of all types, coordinators, news team, editor, videographer, photographer, girls or boys clubs, (need leaders or mentors) etc.

Some offices are assigned. Make yourself available to those in office or to those who appoint new officers. Present a good appearance with a typed résumé. If you were not assigned to an office, volunteer your services if needed, especially to the leaders. This can open doors for you now and in the future, as well as make you popular.

Walk

Walk with confidence. Try to walk with a good posture. Your back should be erect and relaxed. Your head should be straight, not down. Shoulders should be squared and relaxed. Your knees should be slightly bent. If you cannot walk in this manner because of medical reasons, then just look good and confident. Always appreciate who you are because you are unique.

$\mathcal{W}$alk with confidence

When a man is walking with a woman on the street, it is courteous for a man to walk on the side nearest the traffic or the street. This is shown as a sign of protection and to help keep the lady clean if water were to splash near her. Men will be surprised how most women remember them for something so simple, yet courteous. Women: please allow a man to be courteous. It would not take anything from you. It will only allow him to appreciate and respect you more.

Being Courteous

I grew up in a world where people were courteous. One would **not** forget to say "please," "Sir," "Ma'am," "thank you," "may I," or "you are welcome." Most people nowadays are rude. They do not teach the younger generation to say, "Mr. so and so," or "Mrs., Miss, or Ms. so and so." It is sad to see a little 4 or 7 year-old addressing an adult by their first name without having the courtesy to say Mr. or Miss. Where are the parents? Or are they backwards and lack class?

Adults and young adults need to remind younger ones to address them accordingly. This helps the younger ones to show respect for older folks.

It does not hurt to say "thank you" to someone who was kind enough to let you out of an intersection or who was kind enough to help you. Please be courteous and say "Thank you."

Please, is a word that has become obsolete in the English language. I mean, _helloooo_ everyone! What is so hard in saying "please" to another human being? You are human and I am sure you would like others to show you respect. So, please show respect also. Thank you.

"Please" is not begging. It allows you to show appreciation to others. "May I have that please," should be used in place of "Gim-me that." "May I" is the proper use of the English language.

Were you not taught to greet others when you enter a room? Well, since you were not taught, I am going to give you a chance to be aware of it, or remind you if you have forgotten. When you enter a room and one or more persons are in the room, it is proper to greet them by saying, "Hi, hello, good morning, good afternoon, good day," etc. It shows that you are courteous, intelligent, and well-mannered. People will not only remember you, but they will recall you in a good light. I do not mean when you enter a public facility where many people are gathered. I am talking about a private residence, your friends' home, or small gathering. Please do not forget or do not be afraid to be polite. This will help lead you on the road to being popular. People will remember you. They will in turn, greet you when they see you.

To be courteous does not make you look weak or stupid. In fact, it makes you look smart, good looking, assertive, handsome, pretty and awesome. To be rude is unpopular and weak.

*P*opular people look desirable and smell good.

Hygiene/Outward Appearance

Popular people look desirable and smell good. Taking care of your body is hygienic and sensible. Shower once or twice daily. If you cannot take a shower or bath daily, it is best to wash yourself by using a washcloth with running water over a sink or water in a basin. After showering, be sure to use an underarm deodorant. Also, wash your clothes that you wear weekly and change into clean underwear daily. If you fail to do this, you may have an unpleasant body odor without realizing it, especially if you are an active person. This is also an easy way to develop an illness. Wash or change your workout (exercise) clothes very often. If you sweat easily or are very overweight, try to take the above precautions seriously.

Brush your teeth after every meal. If it is not possible to brush, rinse your mouth with water. Floss regularly. This will help keep your gums healthy. Have regular dental checkups. Keep your breath smelling fresh at all times.

You may save your teeth from cavities by employing these to your daily routine.

A mint candy or mint-chewing gum can temporarily control bad breath. Try not to use chewing gum as an excuse not to brush your teeth. It can become habitual. Check your breath regularly. At times, your breath may have an odor and you may be unaware. However, if your mouth is cared for, you need not worry unless you eat foods with garlic or onions. Drink plenty of fresh clean water daily. Bad breath is one of the easiest ways to turn people away from you no matter how gorgeous and attractive you look.

Hair

Your hair should be clean and styled nicely. Men should get a great haircut or trimmed regularly. Be creative with your hairstyle and choose what is best for you. A colorful head of hair such as orange, blue, red, purple, green, etc., is unnatural and very outlandish. You do not want people to perceive you as an idiot, someone with issues, or a clown when you are not.

Ladies, if you have to wear a weave make it look as natural and lovely as possible. Imitating celebrities by sporting a certain style does not mean it is for you. People in *showbiz* need their kind of wardrobe to present a certain image. Unless you are living that kind of lifestyle, it is best to appear in a good-looking manner.

Women should cut or have their hair trimmed every eight to twelve weeks; it will look a lot better. In addition, too much grease in the hair will cause it to become smelly, dry, and stiff. Try a moisturizing shampoo and conditioner, followed by a hair polish for dry hair. Massage your scalp at night to wake up your sebaceous (oil) gland. If you have bi-racial hair types or curly hair, consider using the products of Mixed Chicks. Go to www.mixedchicks.net and consider their products. It leaves your hair soft and beautiful with no frizz.

Most men love to see women with long hair, so if possible women should wear their hair long. Some women are popular because of their long hair. This does not mean that women who wear their short hair will not be recognized. On the contrary, there are women with short hairstyles who are popular because of their dynamic haircut. Remember, your hair is one of the first things people see and admire.

Braids

Men love to see single braids on a woman; it is alluring and beautiful.

Braids are a great asset to those who want a rest from setting or fussing with their hair every day. Africans and people of the East have braided their hair for centuries. They know the blessings of hair braiding. People in today's Western societies have copied one of the oldest forms of hairstyles in the world by braiding their hair. The art of hair braiding is a form of beauty and special skill.

There are many styles that can be achieved. Different styles include:

Conservative, liberated, moderate, short, long, close to the head (cornbraids), away from the head (single or box braids), fish braids or extensions added to cornbraids to create a totally different look. There are girls and women I know who have worn braids in their hair for a period of time (of course, taking it out and re-braiding every several weeks.) whose hair have grown literally down to their backs. Not only were family and friends surprised, but they were surprised too!

The reason why hair tends to grow to a longer length in a shorter period of time when it is braided, is that, there is no constant tugging and combing of the hair. It gets a chance to rest and relax. This allows for little damage, if any, so the hair keeps its length. Once you unbraid your hair and decide that you are not going to wear it in braids for a while, the ends should be cut or trimmed.

Men love to see single braids on a woman; it is alluring and beautiful.

When braids are undone, do not be alarmed if you see a lot of hair coming out because it is estimated that everyone loses about 60 to 70 strands per day. This is normal. (excerpt about hair, from: "How to Grow Long Glorious Hair," by Joan Wright Lewis, info@jovalpub.com)

Dress Your Best

Always try to look your best. You do not have to buy new clothes. The same clothes can be rotated and worn with different accessories and could make a big difference, i.e. a different color tie, belt, shirt, blouse, scarf, handbag, socks, hose, shoes, etc. If you look nice, you should smell nice as well. Wear cologne, perfume, body splash, etc

Practice to look your best. Check out the latest trend in fashion magazines. If you cannot buy a magazine, go to the library. The library is filled with a variety of magazines. If you cannot afford the new clothes, use what is in your closet and imitate the new fashions. You may also set your own fashion trends. Do you like to design new clothes? Copyright your work first, and then send it to the fashion editors of fashion magazines. You may start a new trend. If they accept your work and highlight you in their magazine, that would be awesome for you. This would absolutely make you popular.

Looking your best does not mean you have to be dressed up all the time. Ladies, a simple pair of jeans or skirt that was washed and ironed along with a feminine blouse and hair pulled back is lovely and simple. Men, a pair of jeans, khaki or corduroy (not showing your underwear or butt) along with a tee shirt or a collared shirt is great. Portray yourself with dignity and a pleasant atmosphere around you.

Please do not allow your stomach to show or hang out, especially if you do not have a flat stomach. There is nothing more unbecoming than to see a lovely or handsome face and then your mid-drift is bulging out as if you are pregnant. Dress decent and cover up. If you have a beautiful flat stomach, school and office

*A*lways try to look your best.

is not the place to show it. Remember you are trying to be popular, not unpopular.

Kindness and Caring

To be kind and caring is a fine art. When one is of this nature, it draws people to him or her. Yes, people like to be treated well. To say unkind words to others, or call people names, even if they are children, is wrong. Unkind words may be abusive to the hearer. Do not say words you would not like spoken to you. Do not be mean to others. You will be hated. They will not want to see you or be around you. People will always remember someone that they want to be like and emulate.

Friendliness and Admiration

The book of Proverbs in the Bible says in order for someone to have friends he must be friendly. One of the prerequisites to being popular is friendliness. We are attracted to those who are friendly.

A friendly person is not afraid to say "Hi," with a genuine smile. Also, a nice honest compliment is a complete plus. You may say an admiring comment if someone's hair looks lovely or he is wearing a nice tie, or she a beautiful dress or shoes. Compliment if he or she has lovely glowing skin, nicely shaped eyes, a lovely smile, or is intelligent, smart and a great cook. Perhaps he or she is good at sports. Do not pass up the opportunity to tell others the precious things you notice about them. People love to be complimented, and will adore you. This will make you popular.

If he has gorgeous strong looking muscles, or a six, or an eight-pack, tell him. But never flatter anyone. Stop before you say anything and look at the person. You may see or remember something truthful about them.

People love to be admired. Men especially, appreciate when women admire their

If he has gorgeous strong looking muscles, a six or an eight-pack, tell him.

masculinity. But remember what was just mentioned above. Be honest in your admiration of others. If a man is thin as a beanpole and you say "I like your strong looking muscles," who are you kidding? Certainly not him! Look for other things to admire. Maybe he smiles nicely or dresses well. Perhaps he is skillful at making things with his hands, or he is good at sports, or speaks well, etc. There are many things to admire about each human being. God blessed each one of us with something unique about ourselves. Admiration lets one feel good about one's self. It makes one feel valuable. When you admire others, they will always be happy to see you because you make them feel good about themselves.

Encouragement

It is good to encourage others; even the person you think is dumb or you are jealous of. Encouragement and admiration give the person a sense of personal worth. They will really like having you around. You will be remembered in a nice way. If a friend puts you down and

*A*lways appreciate who you are because you are unique.

makes you feel bad most of the time, that person is not a true friend. It is best for you to be around friends that uplift your spirit and make you feel good about yourself.

Making fun of someone or laughing at them because the majority is doing so is very unwise. Not only will you discourage that person, but he/she will hate being around you. They will be very disheartened. Some people have come back and killed those who were mean to them. So be very careful of the way you treat others. Be kind.

One of the most encouraging and popular persons now and in the past is Jesus Christ. He was so popular during His time on earth that the authorities in His time were intimidated by His popularity. He was loving and kind and in touch with His Father, God. People flocked to see Him from many different places. There were times He did not get a chance to sleep. They followed Him almost everywhere. There were times He asked the people to leave because He needed to be refreshed. They left reluctantly and returned the following day. He was such a great blessing and encouragement to them. The authorities were so jealous they killed him. But even though he was killed, he was still popular, because His death was a part of God's plan for the salvation of man. He died because He loved people. He rose from the dead on the third day and later ascended back to heaven.

There are those of us who can be kind, loving, and popular as Jesus *is*. You see, Jesus is still encouraging those who are discouraged. Those who accept His encouragement should encourage others.

You can read about the life of Jesus Christ in the "Bible," the four gospels – Matthew, Mark, Luke, and John. There is also a book titled "The Desire of Ages" by Ellen G. White. This is an excellent portrayal of the life of Jesus Christ. It is a great love story. I have read this book several times and have learned from it how to love, care, and encourage others. You can read about His life. It may help you to be an encouragement to others and yourself. Ask your favorite bookstore to order it, order from amazon.com, or write to: Review and

Herald Publishing Association, 55 West Oak Ridge Drive, Hagerstown, MD 21740.

Acceptance

Do not try to change anyone. It will drive them away. If you do not like their personality, then stop being around them or learn to accept them. If you do not want to lose his/her friendship, let the person know how you feel. Also, check yourself. Perhaps there is something about you that is evoking such reaction. You may notice a difference in his/her reaction after you have made the necessary changes. However, if the person wants you to be like them or do what they do, please DO NOT let anyone lead you into doing anything that you believe is wrong.

Reassurance & Understanding

Everyone needs reassurance and understanding. Everybody make mistakes; no one is perfect. If someone is behaving weirdly or acting out of the norm, ask what is wrong. Perhaps something is not right with them. Try to understand the person and reassure when needed. Sometimes all someone needs to hear is a simple reassurance like, "You can make it;" "You have the ability to be what you want;" "You are pretty;" "God has blessed you with a wonderful talent, use it;" "Cheer up, I am here if you need me;" "You look great;" "I love you;" "God will see you through," and so on.

Reassurance and understanding make it easier a person to grow. It helps them to feel good about themselves. When you let someone feel good, they value your company. And your friendship will be appreciated, too.

Wrong? Apologize

If you did something wrong, correct it and learn to apologize. If you are wrong about something, do not be afraid to say you are wrong. It takes a big and mature personality to apologize. Humbling yourself makes you appear as a stronger and better person. People will trust

𝕸en love to see women with long hair

and respect you for it. If you have problems apologizing, ask God to help you.

Listening

Learn to listen when someone is speaking. Give your undivided attention. People love when others listen to them. They will always seek your company. Remember not to interrupt until they have finished speaking. Also, never allow a conversation to become one-sided unless the other party is hurting and needs mental relief.

Helpful

It is nice to be helpful without letting anyone take advantage of you. You can gain friends and popularity. Helpfulness shows that you are willing to go out of your way because you care about the person.

Intelligence

You should read to develop your mind. Brain-developing books can open your mind to many new and exciting things. Those who read only comics, romance, thrillers, and mystery books keep their mind closed and addicted to those subjects.

By reading an assortment of good books, you will be exposed to many topics and a wide variety of subjects. You will find books and magazines that uplift the soul, teach wondrous things about our world, and instruct how to treat each other with love and respect. There are also books that teach about the love of God for us. You will discover books about history, science, politics, health, love, food, home and marriage, sex, romance, relationship, business and arts, etc.

The Bible is an excellent book to read. It contains a wealth of knowledge and covers a wide range of topics. You can also gain much from other people's experiences. You can learn through life's trials and experiences. The

Internet, radio, television, and newspaper have a wealth of knowledge. Schools and libraries abound with excellent materials also. Take time out and read, read, read! The more knowledgeable you are about a subject, the more people will want to hear from you.

Public Speaking

When you possess a wealth of knowledge you will be a more interesting person. If you are knowledgeable about a particular subject, you could conduct seminars at various places, carry out tele-seminars on the Internet, or write a book. This would definitely launch you on the road to popularity. Knowledge teaches humility, because the more you learn, the more you realize how much you do not know.

Read as much information about public speaking or take a course if you need to be more confident. Public speaking assures popularity. President Barack Obama did many public speeches. This made him very popular. He also did research on his topic so he could be confident in front of the public. He was always prepared. When you speak in front of the public, you should always be ready, even if it is impromptu.

You could choose from a range of topics to speak about. Remember, this is the information age. If you are knowledgeable about a particular topic, you could teach others about it. You may conduct your topics through seminars, YouTube, tele-seminars (Internet), workshops, conferences, speeches, classroom assignments, etc. You will be popular because you are up front and in the public's eye. If you are in school, do not be afraid to respond to questions and speak up in class.

If you attend a church, temple, or a synagogue, volunteer to teach a Sunday or Sabbath school class. Make sure you read and study the Bible lessons for the class you are teaching. Write down interesting question you would like to ask the class. This would allow them to participate and enjoy the class more. I have taught in church school classes since I was about fourteen years-old, and it has helped me tremendously to speak up. Join and lead out as a

You should read to develop your mind
and your vocabulary.

Scout or Pathfinder leader. I volunteered to lead out with the youth. This made me very popular. Do not be afraid to volunteer and lead out. Never belittle yourself. You have talents and abilities to be of help to others.

Jealousy

Jealousy is an important emotion, and should be handled carefully. It may cause great pain, especially if taken too far. It can cause a person to think irrationally. Jealousy is an emotion that as soon as it creeps upon us, we must try our best to eradicate it completely. It could cause conflict, crimes of all sort, hatred, and even murder.

Jealousy is an emotion that if not controlled, can lead a person to do things that they would not normally do. The feeling of jealousy is very strong and may cause a person to want to do something to destroy the other person.

Pride, low self-esteem, and fear can open the door to envy and jealousy. The Bible says, "Let us have no self-conceit, no provoking of one another, no envy of one another (Galatians 5:26)." Instead of becoming jealous of a person, get to know him or her. Jesus asked us to love one another as we love ourselves. In 1st Corinthians 13:4, it says, "Love is patient and kind; love is not jealous or boastful." When we love someone as ourselves, we have no room to be jealous of them.

We must develop a good and healthy self-esteem by loving and being kind to ourselves. We must pamper ourselves sometimes, and perhaps even hug ourselves. We should appreciate our God-given beauty and come up with ideas on how to accept or improve the things that we are not satisfied about ourselves. Once we have developed a good self-esteem, we feel good about who we are. When someone comes along by whom we feel threatened, we will know how to handle ourselves with the unwanted feelings of jealousy. Look to God for strength and answers.

When we love someone as ourselves,
we have no room to be jealous of them.

Jealousy can stem from many things. Our childhood has a lot to do with the many jealousies that creep into our lives. Our parents have great influence over us. They shape the way we feel about things, people and ourselves. Some of these influences may have been good or bad. We should choose wisely the good influences. We must be thankful for whom we are and the blessings God has imparted to us.

Do not allow anyone to make you feel resentful or envious. If someone has something that you wish you had, do not envy that person. Be happy with what you have or have accomplished. You must feel good about yourself. If your parents were negative, seek the Lord and ask Him to make you feel positive about yourself, and to be happy with whom you are. There is only one you, and there is no one else like you. We are all similar and, at times, experience similar problems. Nonetheless, each person is unique and special.

Do not hate someone because they have better things (a job, spouse, car, more friends, bigger breasts, bigger buttocks, long sexy legs,

121

long wavy, straight, or curly hair, six pack abs) than you or they are prettier than you are, or have a bigger or nicer house than yours. You are being unfair to you and that person. That person may be unhappy and they may be going through bad experiences that you know nothing about. However, if they are happy, be happy for them. Also, remember that beauty is in the eyes of the beholder. You may think someone is better looking than you are, and someone else thinks you are prettier than that person. Ladies, a soft, pleasant attitude is always welcomed. When you feel good about yourself and look for the good in others, you are using a stepping-stone to crush the feelings of jealousy. (Jealousy, from "Secrets to a Romantic Relationship")

Be yourself

Do not imitate anyone. Be yourself. If you have bad habits, try to get rid of them. Ask God to get rid of it, and try your best through Him to let it go. Remember, you are unique and special. Really, stop and think about it: you are very, very special. There is no one else like you, no matter how similar things may seem. You have special talents.

Consider this: you may have a beautiful smile, a certain twinkle in your eye, a cute or nice walk. Perhaps you have a unique way to play the guitar or a special way to sing. Maybe you are a counselor, a musician, or a writer. You may have leadership ability or pose well for photographs. Many things make you special. Maybe you sew well, or you love animals. Perhaps you have good business sense, have a bubbly and a great personality, etc. As you try to be you, love yourself and learn to love others as well.

There are many things that make you special. Maybe you
sew well, or you love animals.

Love yourself

God made you in His image. You are precious. Christ died on the cross for every human being in this world. Remember God said, "The wages of sin is death." We sinned; we are supposed to die forever. However, He died in our place, so we could have a chance to live with Him in heaven, forever. If you were not important, he would not have died for you and then rose on the third day. You have the ability through His power to do and become what he made you to be, and to be a blessing to others. The dreams and talents you have are a part of you. God gave these gifts to you. Accept who you are. You are royalty, because God is your Father and He created you.

It does not matter what anyone has said to you. You are an awesome creation. Accept yourself; you are worth it. How do I know this, even though I may not know you? You are a human being, created in the image of the Great Almighty Monarch of the universe. Therefore, you are one of a special kind. You have the right to love yourself.

From this point forward, you must ask God to let you obey Him. Trust in the abilities He has given you. Put your best foot forward. When the down times show its ugly face, squash it and pick yourself up, and move forward through His power. Look in the mirror and say to yourself:

"I am lovely."

"I am beautiful."

"I am gorgeous."

"I am fabulous."

"I am handsome."

"I am good looking

"I am smart."

"I am intelligent."

"I am strong."

"I am worth it."

"I am talented."

"I am wealthy."

"I am a child of God, therefore, I am royalty."(a prince or a princess)

"I am created in the image of God, the most powerful being in the universe."

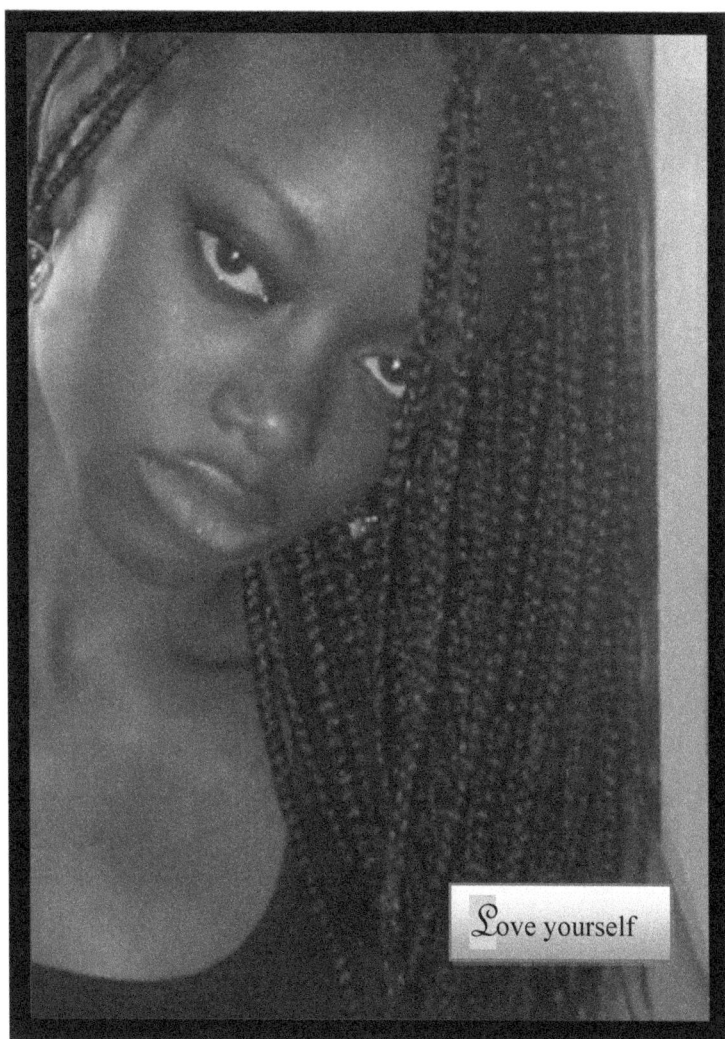

Love yourself

Believe what you are saying. It may seem hard at first, but rehearse saying it daily, believing. Practice! Practice! Practice! Yes, you are worth it, you are special -- you are precious. You have the power to change your mindset (your attitude). Take a half-hour out daily and practice.

Good Leadership

Leaders are usually popular. A leader does not have to lead in an organization. The leader may lead out in a small group of two or three to thirty people. It may be a group of friends or an organization. If you have the potential to be a leader, sharpen your leadership skills by reading good materials that will teach you how to be a good leader.

<u>A Good Leader</u>

❖ A good leader should be caring, patient, creative, calm, understanding, intelligent, assertive, and encouraging.

❖ A good leader listens and then speaks intelligently. Is careful of what he/she say and how it comes across. Is not judgmental.

❖ A good leader is friendly and trustworthy.

❖ A good leader accepts others as they are and encourages them to move forward.

❖ A good leader tries their best to be a good role model. People look up to inspiring leaders.

❖ A good leader does not force anyone to do something that the individual does not want to do.

❖ A good leader has the ability to serve others and change circumstances or ideas.

❖ A good leader does not gossip.

❖ A good leader trusts God to lead.

❖ And remember, a good leader does **NO SUBSTANCE ABUSE!!!!!! No Drugs.**

$\mathcal{T}$here is no one else like you. No matter how similar
things may seem.

Assertiveness

Do not be afraid to speak your mind carefully and intelligently. Be careful of your tone of voice, your choice of words, and the way it is said. You may say things in a certain way that can cause hurt or misunderstanding. This may start an argument and/or drive people away. The words you use, especially if you are angry, may cause great pain to someone. You may feel good at the moment you are saying it, but you may be very sorry later. Calm down and sort things through your mind before you speak. Speak with confidence. Stand your ground graciously. Go after what you want, as long as it will not hurt anyone. Do not be afraid to take on a challenge without being aggressive or mean. Be strong and courageous. Strength is not necessarily aggression. Strength is confidence and patience.

Do not let people push you around, even if you feel fearful. Stand up to them. You are worth it.

Activities

If you attend school, college, church, temple, or are in a good organization, try to take part in some or all of the activities that take place. You will meet people, it will be a learning opportunity, and you will have fun. You will be seen and heard. Also, if you are the kind of person who likes to be seen out in public, you should get a job that will put you up front where people will be around you.

Most people tend to be followers. So, wherever people gather, be it at a party, a meeting or a get-together, if there are no leaders, try to lead out. Maybe the host or hostess is shy, busy, or tired. See what you can do to get things started. You can start conversations or activities. Do not be afraid to lead out. You will be surprised how people react or listen to you. Most people are willing to have someone take the lead. If they refuse to do anything, they may be shy, so do not give up. This will open the door to popularity.

Find out all the
information you
need for the career
of your choice and
go for it.

A Career

One of the best ways to become popular is to have a career in the limelight. Some careers that can put you in the spotlight are: acting, modeling, photography, singing, dancing, comedy, politics, instructor, make-up artist, publisher, fashion designer, minister, writer, cosmetologist, editor, columnist, artist, any sports-related, author, broadcasting (which includes radio and television), film, or movie producer. The Internet will also open doors, but be very careful and alert when surfing the web. Do not give out personal information to strangers; even if you have been talking to them for weeks. Find out all the information you need for the career of your choice and go for it. Do not say it is impossible. Others have lived and experienced it, and so can you.

Conclusion

The preceding information works. I know, because my phone rings often. There are times when I am very busy talking to people. There are times I am unable to return their calls. When I was in college, a student approached me and said, "You know, you are one of the most popular girls on campus." She even knew my name and I did not know her. Another day I took a long walk around campus with a friend. As we came to the end of our walk he said, "Every person we passed today knew you. I knew you know a lot of people on campus, but I didn't realize you were so popular." I was not even aware of my popularity until he mentioned it. I loved and cared about those around me. People are attracted to good people; people that they want to be like.

What keeps me going in this life is the fact that I know and trust in Jesus Christ. I pray to God daily. I ask for His protection and for Him to make me a better person. If you have any problems in your life, try God. You will have a more peaceful and happy life. Ask Him to give you joy, peace and happiness. I hope the best for you.

NEVER give up because you are very Special, especially to God. Remember you are on God's mind and you have the ability to do what you want. So go ahead and live your dreams, and be popular!

☺

INDEX

Index

Give a Gift to a
Friend or Family Member

CHECK YOUR FAVORITE BOOKSTORE OR ORDER NOW

☐ Yes, please send _____ copies of *How to Be Popular* at $16.95 each, plus $4.95 shipping per book (Indiana residents please add 7% sales tax per book). Orders over 5 books or more is discounted at $11.95 each, plus $2.95 shipping per book. (IN 7% sales tax.) Allow 14 days for delivery.

My check or money order is enclosed for the amount of
$_____
My mailing address is:

Name: _____

Address: _____

City: _____ State: _____ Zip: _____

Telephone: _____

Email address:_____

Please make your check payable and return to:
Jo-Val Publishing
8485 Robin Run Way
Avon, Indiana 46123

Call for discounts on large orders
Call credit card orders to 1-317-272-1060
Email: info@jovalpub.com
Faster orders, visit our website: www.jovalpub.com

Author, Wright Lewis, born in Jamaica, is now a citizen of the US. She graduated from Forest Hills High, in Queens, NY, then attended Atlantic Union College, in So. Lancaster, MA; has written *Destini the Chocolate Princess* and other books. She conducts relationships seminars for those wanting a happier relationship. Wright Lewis now lives in Indiana with her husband and children.